TO:

Sweet Madeline

FROM:

Aunt Jody

DATE:

12/2022

Advent is a time to reflect on God's promises and to anticipate the fulfillment of those promises! I hope this book blesses your 2023 Advent season! ♡ J!

The WONDER OF CHRISTMAS

25 Days of Advent Journaling for girls

SHANNA NOEL

WITH DARCY PATTISON

DaySpring

LIVE YOUR FAITH

The Wonder of Christmas: 25 Days of Advent Journaling for Girls
Copyright © 2019 DaySpring Cards, Inc. All rights reserved.
Artwork © 2019 Shanna Noel. Used by permission.
First Edition, November 2019

Published by:

P.O. Box 1010
Siloam Springs, AR 72761
dayspring.com

Written by: Darcy Pattison
Cover & Interior Design by: Shanna Noel

Printed in China
Prime: J1592
ISBN: 978-1-64454-441-9

CONTENTS

FAMILY

All nations on earth will be blessed because of You.
GENESIS 12:3

IN the fullness of time—at the right time in the history of the universe—a baby was born. It was a humble birth in a stable, with only animals to welcome the baby. Yet that moment changed everything. It was a surprising and earth-shattering advent.

An advent is the arrival of a notable person, event, or thing. The Christmas Advent season includes the four Sundays leading up to Christmas and celebrates the arrival of baby Jesus. As you start this Advent journal, think about Jesus's family. His forefathers include Abraham, Moses, and King David. It includes Rahab, Ruth, and Bathsheba. His family was made up of kings, queens, prophets, loyal foreigners, a "man after God's own heart," and courageous women of faith.

Years before Jesus's birth, God promised that "all nations on earth would be blessed" through Abraham's children. That means that Jesus would be a blessing to all people. But it also means that you, a child of God, will be a blessing to others.

day ONE

ALL NATIONS ON EARTH WILL BE BLESSED

Think about your own family—your mother, father, and grandparents. Your family is amazing too! Do you know what each of your family members has accomplished? Spend time talking with them about the things they've done in their lives.

Start this happy season by journaling your gratitude to your parents and grandparents for raising you to know God and His love. Gratitude means thankfulness and a heart that remembers the good things others have done for you.

PRAYer:

Lord, help me to become skilled in both crafts and gratitude. May my words and art be pleasing to You and bring You glory.

Creative Spark

In the space below, write about your family— your parents and grandparents—and use your words to describe what they mean to you.

....

....

....

....

....

....

....

....

day
ONE

Express your gratitude for your family through art. You can draw, paint, or use stickers to show your love for your family.

FAMily

Often we see lots of family during the Christmas season. Before a family gathering, pray for each family member. At the gathering, ask questions about their current year and their hopes for the next year. Plan to pray consistently for them during the year to come.

Draw your family tree.

BELiEVE

Right away Zechariah could speak again.
Right away he praised God.
LUKE 1:64

(READ ZECHARIAH'S WHOLE STORY:
LUKE 1:5-25, 39-45, 57-66.)

ZECHARIAH and Elizabeth were faithful worshipers of God. Zechariah was a priest. They both "did what was right in the sight of God. They obeyed all the Lord's commands and rules faithfully" (Luke 1:6). Their only sadness was that they had never had a child. When their story is told in Luke 1, they were "very old." There wasn't much hope of children.

One day, Zechariah was chosen to burn incense in the inner court of the temple. An angel appeared to him there. The angel said that Zechariah and Elizabeth would have a son and he should be called John. Zechariah's baby would grow up to be John the Baptist, the prophet who preached in the wilderness and baptized Jesus. But Zechariah couldn't see the future. He only saw that he and his wife were very old.

Zechariah was unsure of himself and the situation. He argued

with the angel. The angel then did something drastic. He told Zechariah that he wouldn't be able to speak until the baby was born. Zechariah came out of the holy place of the temple and couldn't talk for almost ten months. When his son was born, Elizabeth wanted to name the baby John. Usually boys were named after someone in the family, and no one held the name of John in their family. Zechariah still couldn't talk, so he wrote, "His name is John." And suddenly Zechariah could speak again.

The Bible says, "Right away he praised God" (Luke 1:64). Zechariah had changed. At first he doubted the angel's prophecy. But when he saw the prophecy come true, Zechariah praised God.

Believing is a choice. Zechariah is described as a man who "did what was right in the sight of God" (Luke 1:6). He obeyed the commandments and rules. But when he was faced with an angel, he didn't believe.

PRAYer:

Father, the Bible gives many promises to believers.
Help me to choose to believe that the promises are true.

BELiEVE

Zechariah didn't believe the angel. He didn't believe that God could give an old man and woman a baby. He didn't believe that God could do a miracle.

Believing is a choice. When faced with believing the impossible, do you believe what God is telling you through the Bible? Write your answer below.

BELiEVE

I believe in...

day
TWO

Write, paint, and journal about choosing to believe.

I BELiEVE IN

ANGELS

In the sixth month after Elizabeth had become pregnant, God sent the angel Gabriel to Nazareth, a town in Galilee. He was sent to a virgin. The girl was engaged to a man named Joseph. He came from the family line of David. The virgin's name was Mary. The angel greeted her and said, "The Lord has blessed you in a special way. He is with you."

LUKE 1:26-28

IMAGINE an angel appearing to you. Would you be confused? Disturbed? Mary was definitely scared when the angel spoke to her. He told her some surprising things: although she was a virgin, she was going to have a baby boy who would rule over God's people forever.

Would you argue with an angel? Like Zechariah, Mary questioned the angel. The surprise is that the angel didn't get mad. Instead, he took the time to explain things. (Read Luke 1:26-38 for the whole conversation.)

An angel also appeared to Joseph in a dream, saying, "Don't be afraid to take Mary home as your wife" (Matthew 1:20-21). In other words, God directly spoke to this young man and his wife. Scared or not, Mary and Joseph believed Him, while Zechariah didn't.

Day Three

Does God want to speak to you? Yes! The Bible is your love letter from God. Through Scripture, God can speak to your heart about what is troubling you or making you excited.

Both the Bible and angels are messengers that speak words of life. God has given us stories and wise words in the Bible. It's a useful tool that helps us in four ways (II Timothy 3:16):

1. the Bible is useful for deciding what is true or false;

2. the Bible is useful to fix our mistakes;

3. the Bible is useful to make our lives whole; and

4. the Bible is useful to train us to do what is right.

What if you treated the Bible as if it were an angel speaking to you?

PRAYer:

O God, I'm amazed that You care enough
to speak to me through the Bible.
Thank You for caring about me that much.
Help me to remember my daily Bible reading.

Creative Spark

USE THE SPACE BELOW to write SOMEthing GOD hAS tOLD you...

"

"

One way the Bible describes angels is "servants like flames of fire" (Hebrews 1:7 NLT). The world pictures angels as plump cherubs or men wearing robes and wings. How would you picture a servant like "flames of fire"? Draw, paint, or color what you imagine an angel looking like in the space below.

HEARING FROM GOD

Interview your family and ask them how God speaks to them. Write each person's name on the line below and then draw their answers in the boxes.

_____
Name

Name

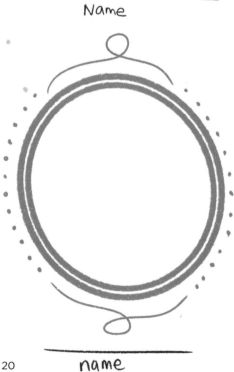

name

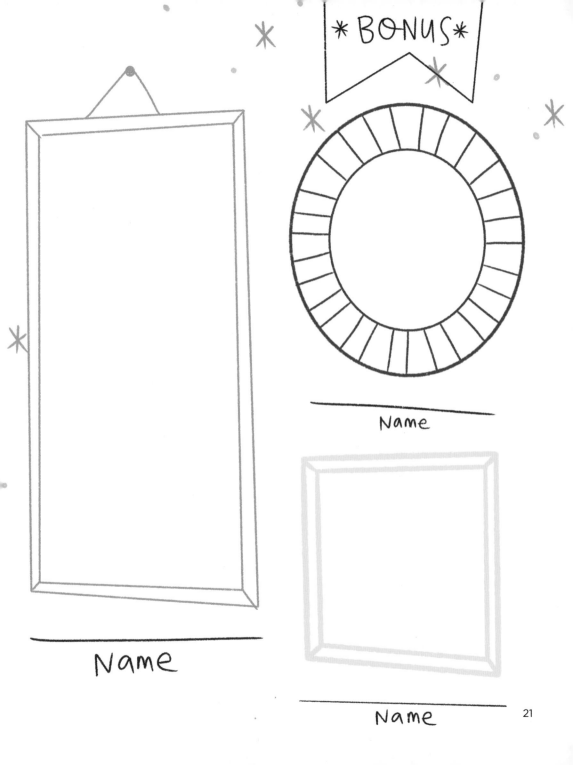

BONUS

Name

Name

Name

21

MIRACLE BABIES

But why is God so kind to me?
Why has the mother of my Lord come to me?
LUKE 1:43

MARY'S pregnancy was a miracle. Elizabeth's pregnancy was a miracle. One was young, and the other was old. But they were connected by their miraculous pregnancies. Mary knew all about Elizabeth and Zechariah's miracle baby. They were "very old," and yet Elizabeth was expecting. When an angel told Mary that she'd have a baby too, it was natural to think of Elizabeth. Together, their sons would change the world.

But Elizabeth and Mary were also connected by family. They were cousins.

Mary had a hard time after becoming pregnant by God. People thought the worst. Likely one reason Mary went to see her cousin was because people were gossiping about her. Gossip, or talking about someone without knowing all the facts, is always harsh. At Elizabeth's house, though, Mary found peace. When Mary entered the house, Elizabeth's unborn baby leaped for joy. Elizabeth said, "You are a woman God has blessed. You have believed that the

day Four

Lord would keep His promises to you!" (Luke 1:45).

Elizabeth was an encouragement to Mary! Elizabeth recognized Mary's faith and obedience. She knew that God had given the baby to Mary. Also, Elizabeth was about six months ahead of Mary in her own pregnancy. That meant she could help Mary understand how carrying a baby would change her body. They had a lot to talk about: pregnancy, baby names, and their faithful God!

Every family has hard times. When that happens to your family, think of Elizabeth the encourager.

If you're interested in Jesus's family tree, read Matthew 1:1–17. It's fun to look up some of the people in the Bible and see what they did for God.

PRAYer:

Father, let me see my family as a blessing from You—even during the hard times. Give me opportunities to encourage each family member during the holidays. I want to be the family's encourager.

In the space below, write the names of all your living relatives. Beside each name, write something encouraging. Plan ways you can give them encouragement during the holidays.

Draw a picture of the people you are most excited to see this Christmas and write out the encouraging words you're going to say to them when you see them.

I ♡ thESE PEOPLE

encourage

66

99

25

MARY'S MAGNIFICAT

Mary was pregnant when she went to see her cousin
Elizabeth. After Elizabeth's encouragement, Mary
praised God in a beautiful song. This is usually called
Mary's Magnificat. In Latin, *magnificat* means "magnifies."
Mary is magnifying or praising God for the coming child.

Mary said,
"My soul gives glory to the Lord.
   My spirit delights in God my Savior.
He has taken note of me
   even though I am not considered important.
From now on all people will call me blessed.
   The Mighty One has done great things for me.
   His name is holy.
He shows His mercy to those who have respect for Him,
   from parent to child down through the years.
He has done mighty things with His powerful arm.
   He has scattered those who are proud in their deepest thoughts.
He has brought down rulers from their thrones.
   But he has lifted up people who are not considered important.
He has filled with good things those who are hungry.
   But He has sent away empty those who are rich.
He has helped the people of Israel, who serve Him.
   He has always remembered to be kind
to Abraham and his children down through the years.
   He has done it just as He promised to our people of long ago."

Highlight a passage from *Mary's Magnificat* on the left, and create art to represent how the Scripture makes you feel.

NAMES OF JESUS

She is going to have a son. You must give him the name Jesus.
That's because He will save His people from their sins.
The virgin is going to have a baby. She will give birth to a Son.
And He will be called Immanuel."...
The name Immanuel means "God with us."
MATTHEW 1:21, 23

(YOU CAN READ MORE ABOUT THE STORY OF
HOW JOHN THE BAPTIST WAS NAMED IN LUKE 1:57–65.)

WHEN John and Jesus were named, it was at the command of God. The angel told Zechariah to name his son *John*. Mary and Joseph were told to call their son *Jesus.*

Here are some things done in "the name of Jesus."

- When the name of Jesus is spoken, everyone will kneel down to worship Him (Philippians 2:10).

- After hearing this, they were baptized in the name of the Lord Jesus (Acts 19:5).

- To a crippled man: "In the name of Jesus Christ of Nazareth, get up and walk" (Acts 3:6).

- "[The apostles] considered it an honor to suffer shame for the name of Jesus" (Acts 5:41).

- "We pray this so that the name of our Lord Jesus will receive glory through what you have done" (II Thessalonians 1:12).

Jesus's name carries power, inspires hearts, endures suffering, and points to God's love. That's just His name! Think about how Jesus is so much more than His name.

What does your name mean? We don't often think about our names—a name is just what everyone calls you. Names can't control you or determine your future, of course. But names are actually part of your identity. There was once a woman named Erin Amelia. Growing up, she was called Amelia. But when she went into the military, she started using her first name, Erin. She didn't change. And yet changing to her first name said something important about her. She was a grown-up now.

What does your name mean to others? What does it mean to you?

PRAyer:

He calls His own sheep by name and leads them out (John 10:3). Father God, I'm amazed that You know my name. Call me and lead me in the path of righteousness! I want to follow You.

Take the time to look up the meaning(s) of your name. What do you think about your name? Do you consider it to be adventurous, calm, happy, excitable, faithful. . . ? As you journal today, consider your name and how it says something special about you.

My NAME :)

My Name is: adventurous ○

happy ○   excitable ◉

calm ○   faithful ◉

Doodle your name along with symbols and icons that represent its meaning.

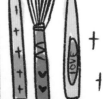

Your DOODLE SPACE! ♡ ♡

JESUS the SAVior

She is going to have a Son.
You must give Him the name Jesus.
That's because He will save His people from their sins.
MATTHEW 1:21

THE ADVENT, or coming, of Jesus—His arrival on earth—was the high point of God's plans. Adam and Eve sinned in the garden of Eden by disobeying God. From that moment, God was separated from mankind. As a holy God, He couldn't have anything to do with sin or people who disobeyed. Otherwise, He wouldn't be holy. God loved mankind, though, and He had a plan to save people from their sins.

Because of sin, people deserve punishment. What if someone else was punished in our place for the things we did? God planned for His Son, Jesus, to be punished instead of us! That's the gospel, the good news of the Bible. We can have a relationship with God because Jesus covers our sin. His death on the cross will "save them from their sin."

Joseph probably didn't understand everything the angel said to him. He couldn't look into the future and understand that the

coming baby would die on a cross. He wouldn't have understood what that meant.

Do you understand the gospel, the good news? If not, find someone to talk with today and ask for a deeper explanation. Jesus's birth really is good news, and you deserve to understand it fully. If you do understand, then celebrate the incredible gift from Jesus—you are saved!

PRAYer:

O God,
You love us even though we are sinful people.
Thank You for having a plan to save us from our sins.
Help me to understand Your plan more each day.

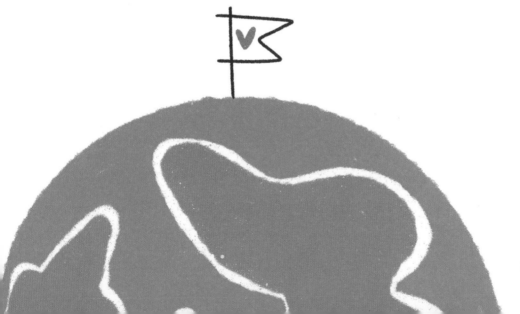

Creative Spark

start

Holidays teach us about God. As the year goes from January to December, we learn different things. Christmas is about Jesus's birth, and Easter is about Jesus's death and resurrection. Today, think about the beginning and ending of Jesus's life. Journal about how endings are connected to beginnings.

end

Think about Jesus's birth in a humble stable and His death on a criminal's cross. Draw and create as you make the connection between the two events and the two holidays.

day
Six

birth

cross

PROPHECY:
BORN in BETHLEHEM

But you, O Bethlehem Ephrathah,
are only a small village among all the people of Judah.
Yet a ruler of Israel, whose origins are in the distant past,
will come from you on my behalf.
MICAH 5:2 NLT

WHEN God has a plan, He makes sure all the details are worked out. The plan for a Savior had many important details. First, God told people exactly where Jesus would be born—in Bethlehem.

About six miles (10 km) south of Jerusalem lies the town of Bethlehem. David was born and raised in Bethlehem. It was there that the prophet Samuel anointed him king.

What does this have to do with God's plans for a Savior? Luke 2:1-4 says that the ruler of the Roman Empire, Emperor Augustus, decided to count how many people lived within its boundaries. This count, or census, required each person to travel to the town of their ancestors and pay a tax. It was a way for the Roman Empire to

day SEVEN

raise money. Joseph, as a descendant of King David, had to go to Bethlehem.

About four hundred years before that, prophets said that the king of the Jews would be born in Bethlehem. To get Joseph and Mary to Bethlehem in time for Jesus's birth, God used the Roman emperor. It wasn't an easy decision for Mary to travel. She was nine months pregnant, almost ready to have her baby. But the Roman emperor said they must go to Bethlehem.

Nothing short of an emperor's decree could make her go on that trip. If she had the baby while on the trip, she'd be away from her mother and family. Going into labor and delivering a baby was hard enough. Doing so in a strange place would be even harder. Yet, the emperor said that they must go. So Mary went with Joseph to Bethlehem to pay the emperor's tax.

The emperor's call for a census and Jesus's birth happened at the same time. Just as God planned.

PRAYer:

Father, I'm amazed that You count every hair on my head. I'm amazed that You care that much about me. Today, let me worry less and trust You more.

Creative Spark

Do you worry about things? Stop! God "counts every hair on your head!" (Matthew 10:30). As you journal today, write down your worries and ask God to give you peace about it all.

DEAR GOD,

day
SEVEN

For Jesus's birth, God had an emperor count the people in his empire. God can easily work out His plans for your life. Draw and create a scene from your life when God did just that.

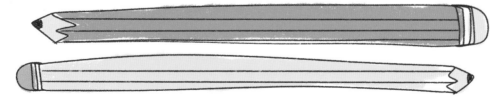

WAITINg

God can do everything!
LUKE 1:37 ICB

NINE months is a long wait for a baby. Mary's wait started when the angel Gabriel told her to expect a son. She spent about three months with her cousin, Elizabeth, in the hill country before returning to Nazareth. The Bible doesn't give details of that time, but we can imagine it. Joseph was worried about marrying her. The baby wasn't his. Her family and friends likely thought she'd been with another man.

Mary told them about the angel and his prophecy. Elizabeth believed her. Most people probably didn't believe her. It was hard to wait for God's Word to come true.

Maybe while she waited, Mary sang this song written by King David: "Wait for the LORD. Be strong and don't lose hope. Wait for the LORD" (Psalm 27:14).

Some people say that God is never late, but He's seldom early. In other words, God does things at exactly the right time—not late and not early. Babies need nine months to grow before they are born. A mother must

day
☆ 8 ☆

wait nine months whether she likes it or not.

Waiting often seems hard to us. We wait for the Christmas holiday to get here. We wait for relatives to arrive. We wait for Christmas parties. We wait for Christmas presents. As we wait, we need to remember that God does things at exactly the right moment. Be strong and don't lose hope. Wait for the Lord!

PRAYeR:

Father, while I'm waiting
for Christmas to come,
help me see the needs of others.

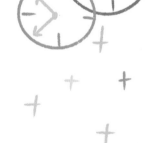

Waiting is a strange in-between time. Look around your neighborhood and find someone who needs help. Could you help with yard work or housework? If you are busy with good deeds, the waiting will go quickly. Journal today about waiting and the things you can do to make time fly.

WHO CAN I HELP ?

Draw and create things you'd rather do than wait on something.

day
☆ 8 ☆

IN the WAIT

WAITING

Waiting doesn't mean sitting back and doing nothing. For a Christian, waiting means doing something: praying and seeking God's will.

....

....

....

....

....

....

....

Use this journal space to draw, paint, color, and write what you are most excited about this upcoming Christmas. What is the hardest thing to wait on this Christmas?

TRAVEL with JESUS

So Joseph went also.
He went from the town of Nazareth in Galilee to Judea.
That is where Bethlehem, the town of David, was.
LUKE 2:4

BEFORE Jesus was born, Joseph and Mary traveled about 80 miles (130 km) from Nazareth to Bethlehem. We don't know whether they walked all the way or had a donkey to ride or to carry packs. We don't know the exact route, but any route meant they climbed over mountains. Scholars estimate that they spent four to ten days on the road. Each night they would have stopped somewhere and asked strangers for a room. They probably wore heavy woolen cloaks to protect them from cold and rain. It's possible that they had to battle wild animals and avoid robbers. It wasn't an easy trip.

When people take a trip, they usually plan a route. They look at maps or mapping apps to decide which roads to take, where to stop for meals, and what time to arrive. As they drive, the mapping

apps give directions on where to turn, updates on traffic, and even weather reports.

When you journey with God through life, the Bible is your map.

Where are you going? To heaven, to be with God.

How do you get there? There are many trails that lead to God and heaven, but they all go through Jesus. God has planned each person's route. You just need to follow His plans.

Read your Bible and listen to God's promptings to find your path.

PRAYer:

Lord, I'm glad that You have
planned the map of my life.
Help my feet not to stray from that path.
I want to follow You.

Creative Spark

Spiritual journeys are unique, but they have common steps along the way. God will guide you along your journey. Even when you get off track (which is totally normal), you can always ask God to show you the next step. In the space below, write about your spiritual journey, when it started, and how you see it leading you to Jesus.

My spiritual journey...

day
NiNe

Draw and create a map of your spiritual journey.

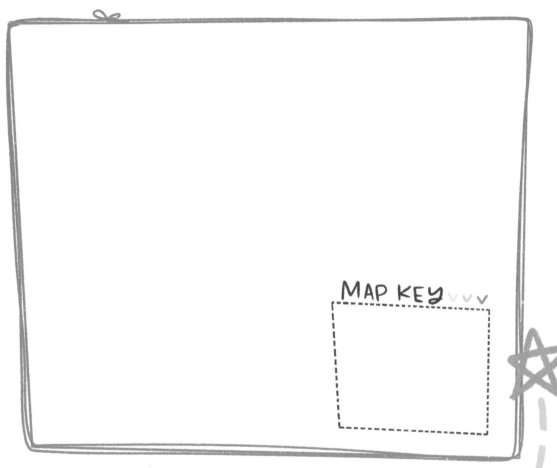

MAP KEY ✓ ✓ ✓

49

SPIRITUAL MAPS

Draw a map of Mary's spiritual journey. Think about these points on the map: the starting point; places where Mary learned to trust God; when Mary obeyed God; where the valleys or hard times of trusting were located; and the ending point—how far it was from the starting point.

Mary's spiritual journey

BONUS

MAP KEY

- ○ _____
- ○ _____
- ○ _____
- ○ _____
- ○ _____
- ○ _____

DISAPPOINTMENT AND
TRUSTING GOD

There were no rooms left in the inn.
LUKE 2:7 ICB

IMAGINE making that long journey from Nazareth to Bethlehem, 80 miles (130 km) away. When you arrive in Bethlehem, it's crowded because others have come to register for the Roman tax too.

If you took a journey like that today, you'd call ahead and book a room at a hotel. If there wasn't room, maybe you'd decide to stay six miles away in Jerusalem. But in those days, there was no phone or internet. You wouldn't know that all the houses and inns were full until you got there.

Tired, hungry, and very pregnant, Mary was probably exhausted. It's hard to trust God when things aren't going your way. When you're sick or grouchy, it's even harder.

James 1:2–3 says, "My brothers and sisters, you will face all kinds of trouble. When you do, think of it as pure joy. Your faith will be tested. You know that when this happens it will produce in you the strength to continue."

day
10

God knows your troubles. Sometimes the troubles are even tests of your faith. Will you pass the test or fail? Anger, grouchiness, disappointment—these emotions are normal. What matters is how you handle the emotions. Will you let bad words come out? Will you treat others badly?

If you pass the test, it will make you stronger. The next time something doesn't go your way, remember that it's a test. Try to overcome the disappointment. Stop the angry words. Thank God that He will strengthen you through the problems.

PRAYer:

Father, when You test my faith with unwanted things, please help me! I want to pass the test. Close my mouth and don't let me say mean things. Make me stronger through the test.

Write about what makes you angry. How do you handle that emotion?

Paint something angry. Use dark colors and make heavy, angry marks. Let your emotions spill out on the page. God knows we have both dark emotions and happy emotions. Don't try to hide your feelings. Let the page dry. Come back later and paint over the angry marks with brighter, happier colors. Sometimes the deep colors and marks will make the finished painting look better.

HUMBLE BEGINNINGS

While Joseph and Mary were in Bethlehem,
the time came for her to have the baby.
She gave birth to her first son.
There were no rooms left in the inn.
So she wrapped the baby with cloths and
laid Him in a box where animals are fed.

LUKE 2:6–7 ICB

BABY showers are parties for new parents. Friends and family give them things they'll need for the new baby: diapers, clothes, furniture, books, a first Bible, and much more. Mary and Joseph didn't get a baby shower. They didn't get to have the baby at home. They didn't get to have grandparents come over and see the baby right away.

Instead, they were out of town, sleeping in a stable. Mary didn't have new clothes for the baby. She took strips of cloth and wound them around Him. She didn't have a beautiful crib or a decorated

nursery. She laid the baby in a manger, the place from which animals eat hay. At least the hay was a soft place to lay the baby, even if the straw would be itchy.

It was a humble beginning for Jesus. The stable was a poor place, a place of low rank. It sure wasn't a castle! The amazing thing is that God likes humility. "He makes fun of proud people who make fun of others. But He gives grace to those who are humble and treated badly" (Proverbs 3:34).

Humility means you don't think of yourself as better than others. Humility builds up others instead of yourself. It doesn't brag. Humility also means being proud of the right things. Mary was proud of her son, but not of His bed. What are you proud of? Where do you need to be humbler?

PRAYer:

Thank You, Lord, for reminding me
that You are to be exalted, not me.
Help me be a servant to others.

Creative Spark

Today, seek out people who need help and cheerfully do something for them. Go to a nursing home and read to someone. Serve food at a soup kitchen. Find a place in your community to help humble people. Afterward, journal about the experience below.

I LOVE TO

Serve

Paint, doodle, or color about your experience.

day
eleven

SHepHerds in their FielDS

There were shepherds living out in the fields nearby.
It was night, and they were taking care of their sheep.
An angel of the Lord appeared to them. And the glory of the Lord
shone around them. They were terrified. . .The shepherds returned.
They gave glory and praise to God. Everything they had seen
and heard was just as they had been told.
LUKE 2:8-9, 20

TODAY'S new parents are excited when their baby arrives. They talk about the baby's weight, length, and name. And if you ask, they'll tell you more—lots more.

In the same way, God was excited that Jesus, His Son, had come to earth. He sent a host of angels to talk to shepherds. Isn't that strange? He didn't tell the priests, or King Herod (the ruler of Judea), or the rich merchants of Jerusalem. Instead, He sent angels to shepherds.

Yesterday, we talked Jesus's humble beginning in a stable. The shepherds were humble folk too. They were probably uneducated and made a living just taking care of sheep. Yet God sent an entire host—that's a bunch of angels—to announce the baby.

The angels frightened the shepherds. But one angel had words to calm them down: "a Savior has been born to you. He is the Messiah, the Lord. Here is how you will know I am telling you the truth. You will find a baby wrapped in strips of cloth and lying in a manger" (Luke 2:11-12).

After talking it over, the shepherds went to Bethlehem and found Mary and Joseph with the baby. The angel's words were true!

The angel said the good news is a "great joy" and it was given "for all the people" (verse 10). But the good news came first to the shepherds. This is one of the many wonders of Christmas. It gives us hope that God will also care about us and our lives.

Peace is promised to "those He is pleased with on earth!" (verse 14). If the promise came to humble shepherds, then you can have peace too. The angel promised it.

PRAYer: Father, thank You for the "great joy" of a Savior. Remind me today, during this busy season, that Jesus is the Reason for the season. Give me peace in the middle of all my busyness.

Below, write a list of people you'd like to tell about God's peace. Try to find time this week to talk with those people and encourage them.

Sheep are funny, wonderful animals. Have fun today with drawing sheep and shepherds.

GOOD NEWS FOR
ALL the EARTh

I have seen your Salvation with my own eyes.
You prepared Him before all people.
He is a light for the non-Jewish people to see.
LUKE 2:30-32 ICB

THE shepherd's story is rich and full of things to think about. Think about the angel's statement: "I bring you good news. It will bring great joy for all the people" (Luke 2:10).

Did the good news come only to shepherds? Only to Israel? Only to believers or Christians? No. "It is for all people." All means "everyone on earth."

This is a great time of year to think about how other people hear about Jesus. Missionaries are people who commit to going somewhere to tell people about the Savior. A missionary may be a person who regularly visits a nursing home to encourage people and tell them about Jesus. Or a missionary may be a person who lives in a certain neighborhood so they can make friends there. Once they make friends in a community, they tell people about Jesus. Some missionaries live overseas on tropical islands with active volcanoes. Why are they risking their lives? They plan to translate the Bible

into a tribal language.

Where is your "mission field"? That is, where has God sent you to tell the good news of peace and joy?

You may protest and say, "I'm just a kid. God wouldn't send me!" But if you're a believer, God does want you to talk about Him! Maybe God wants you to talk to that lonely kid at school. You know—the one who always sits alone at lunch.

Notice the people God puts in your path. Look around. See people as God sees them. He loves each person and wants to save them from their sins.

The "good news of great joy" is "for all the people"!

PRAYer:

Father, thank You that the good news is for all people. Please help Your missionaries to have the strength and courage to tell others about You. Please help me to see people in my world with Your eyes.

Write a list of the people you know who are lonely. God sent His Son, His only Son, to die for that lonely person. He loves them that much. How does God see that person?

Draw or paint people in your life the way God sees them. Learn to see with God's eyes, not your human eyes.

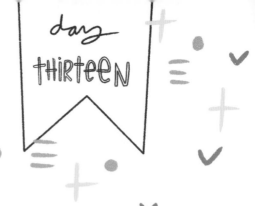

MISSIONARIES

Today, think about a missionary or someone you know who is sharing God's love. In the space to your right, draw their home, the people they minister to, or what you hope for them. It doesn't have to be a missionary in another country. Someone who works in a local ministry or a church is fine. Later, take the time to write them an encouraging note. Missionaries *always* need encouragement.

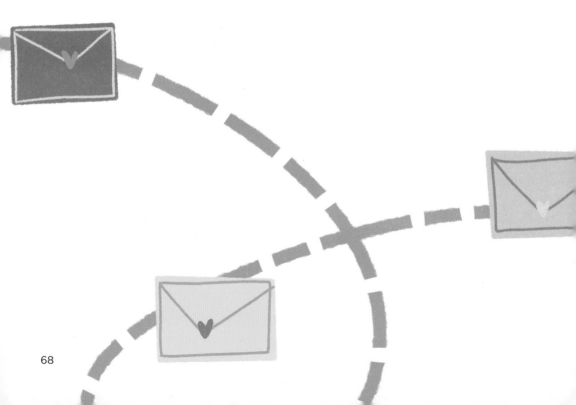

THE SHEPHERDS
TOLD THEIR STORY

After the shepherds had seen Him, they told everyone.
They reported what the angel had said about this Child.
All who heard it were amazed at what the shepherds said to them.
LUKE 2:17–18

THE shepherds were excited. Their night sky had lit up with a host of heavenly angels. They'd heard the good news that a Savior had come. They went to Jerusalem and saw Him. Everything was exactly the way the angel had described it—a baby wrapped up in strips of cloth and lying in a manger. The shepherds worshiped the newborn King.

Okay, now what? What if the shepherds just went back to their fields, yawned, and went to sleep?

That would be crazy! With all that excitement, they should *do* something.

In fact, the shepherds were so excited that they started talking about their amazing night. They acted as television reporters to the people nearby. They lined up the facts and told everything that had happened. They started with the angel's words and then, they told about going to see Jesus themselves.

You do the same thing every day. Something happens—it doesn't have to be a big thing—and you tell someone about it.

"Mom," you say, "I spilled milk all over everyone in the cafeteria."

"Dad," you say, "I got an A on my history test."

It's normal and right to talk about your day. It's also great to tell others about what God has done for you today.

"Mom," you say, "thank you for praying about my headache. The medicine helped, and I had a good day."

"Dad," you say, "I got mad at Angela today. What would Jesus do? Do you think I should call and apologize?"

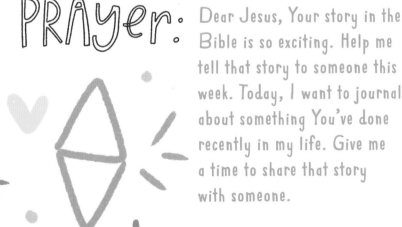

PRAYer: Dear Jesus, Your story in the Bible is so exciting. Help me tell that story to someone this week. Today, I want to journal about something You've done recently in my life. Give me a time to share that story with someone.

Creative Spark

Write a story below about how God has worked in *your* life.

MY STORY ♥

day
14

Use art to tell stories of how God showed up when you needed Him.

A HOST OF ANGELS SINGING

Suddenly a large group of angels from heaven also appeared.
They were praising God. They said,
"May glory be given to God in the highest heaven!
And may peace be given to those He is pleased with on earth!"
LUKE 2:13–14

ANGELS are everywhere in the Christmas story. Angels spoke to Zechariah, Elizabeth, Joseph, Mary, and now to the shepherds. What are angels?

Angels in heaven obey God. Sometimes they are God's messengers, like in the Christmas story. Angels guard the entrance to the garden of Eden and keep men out (Genesis 3:24). Special angels continually worship God (Isaiah 6:3). We know that some angels rule over other angels. Michael is an archangel (Jude 1:9). Gabriel, who spoke to Mary and Zechariah, stands in God's presence and serves Him (Luke 1:19).

We should never worship angels. They serve God, and He expects them to obey Him. They are "mighty

ones" who "carry out His orders and obey His Word" (Psalm 103:20). Instead, we worship God, who created the angels.

"You have come to a joyful gathering of angels. There are thousands and thousands of them" (Hebrews 12:22). We don't know how many angels exist, but we know there are lots of them!

Angels are fascinating to humans. At Christmastime, we often see angel ornaments. A bunch of angels together create a miniature host of heavenly angels. It's a good time of year to think about angels because they are in many places in the Christmas story. Just be careful to worship the baby and not the angels. Only Jesus is worthy of our praise.

PRAYer:

Father God, angels are fascinating
because they are in heaven with You.
Someday, I'll sing Your praises
with the angels in heaven.
Help me to remember to praise You
during this special time of year.

CREATIVE SPARK

What do angels look like? No one knows. On Day 3 of this journal, we learned that in the Bible, angels are described as "servants like flames of fire" in Hebrews 1:7 (NLT). Today, journal about what you know and think about angels.

ANGELS

Draw a "host of heavenly angels." Think of a
night sky above a sheep meadow. How would
that sky look if it was lit up by angels?

ANGELS

Anytime you see an angel during this Christmas season, let it remind you of the message the heavenly host of angels exclaimed: "Do not be afraid. I bring you good news" (Luke 2:10). Let it remind you not to be afraid but to trust Jesus with your whole heart.

BONUS

Design an angel ornament for your tree.

A MOTHER'S HEART

But Mary kept all these things
like a secret treasure in her heart.
She thought about them over and over.
LUKE 2:19

HAVE you ever thought of a memory as a treasure? That it's something valuable to guard? Mary watched God working as Jesus was born. She remembered traveling to Bethlehem, the disappointment of sleeping in a stable, the birth of her first son, the shepherds coming to worship the baby, and the gifts of the wise men. There was a lot to remember. Each step was brought about by God and happened in a unique way.

Mary thought about Jesus's birth over and over. She was meditating on the event. *Meditating* isn't sitting alone in a dark room. Meditating means that you concentrate on something—an event, a question, something you heard—and work to understand it. Christians are told to meditate on Scripture, to fill their heads with His words.

day
Sixteen

Like Mary, you should think "over and over" about what God is teaching you. To help you understand the Scriptures, you may want to read a whole book for the context of a Bible story. Looking up definitions or the background of a biblical person will expand your understanding. Memorizing Scripture is an excellent way to meditate because you must think about every single word. This journal encourages you to think deeply with your creativity and art. You may choose to illustrate a favorite passage from the Bible. After meditating on a Bible verse—however you choose to do it—you'll never forget it. Because meditation hides God's Word in your heart.

PRAYer:

Today, pray this Scripture:
"LORD, may these words of my mouth please You.
And may these thoughts of my heart please You also."
Psalm 19:14

Creative Spark

Write your favorite passages from the Bible in the space below.

♥ this!

I ♥ tHis verse:

Create art today as you meditate on your favorite passages and what they mean to you.

day
SixteeN

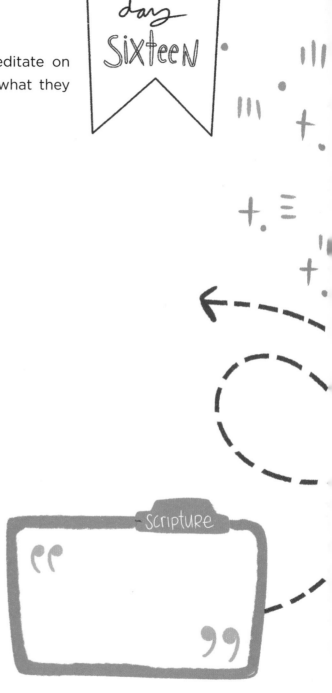

Scripture

" "

CHURCH

So Joseph and Mary took Jesus to Jerusalem.
There they presented Him to the Lord.
In the Law of the Lord it says,
"The first boy born in every family
must be set apart for the Lord."
LUKE 2:22–23

AS NEW PARENTS, Joseph and Mary took Jesus to church when He was just a few weeks old. The temple in Jerusalem was about six miles north of Bethlehem. Traveling with a baby is hard. The baby needs diapers, food, and regular naps. Today, we have bottles, disposable diapers, and car seats. Mary and Joseph had none of that. Instead, one of them would have to carry the baby all the way.

In spite of the problems, traditions of that time said they should take baby Jesus to the temple. Beyond tradition, though, Joseph and Mary believed it was important to obey God.

In Hebrews, Paul reminds us of the importance of going to church: "And let us not give up meeting together. Some are in the habit of doing this. Instead, let us encourage one another with words of hope" (Hebrews 10:25).

Believers should meet together regularly. Usually, this means meeting at a local church where Christians can make friends and get to know other believers. One special thing to do at church is to "encourage one another with words of hope." Going to church isn't about making ourselves feel good. Instead, it's about helping others.

Joseph and Mary took Jesus to church in spite of having to travel with a tiny baby. Compared to them, it's easy for Christians to go to church today. It should be a habit.

PRAYer:

Father, thank You for helping me to learn more about You. Use me to give "words of hope" to others.

Today, write words and phrases that bring you hope. Think through people in your life who might need to be encouraged today.

86

Draw messages or symbols of hope
on the signs below.

CHURCH

The church is bigger than a building. In fact, it isn't a building at all. God is not so concerned with floor plans and constructing walls. He's more concerned with working in and through people.

WHAT CHURCH MEANS TO ME:

Use art to define what a church is.

WONDER
OF GOD'S PLAN

*The Spirit had told Simeon
that he would not die before
he had seen the Lord's Messiah.*
LUKE 2:26

DO you see and understand when God is working in your life? The story of Simeon, a godly man who saw the baby Jesus in the Jerusalem temple, is told in Luke 2:25–35. God had told Simeon that he wouldn't die until he saw the Lord's Christ. Simeon was focused on that promise. He waited and watched for Israel's Savior.

Then one day, God told Simeon to go into the temple courtyard. Here's the amazing thing: Simeon recognized that the baby Jesus was the promised Savior!

Jesus was just a baby, not an adult warrior or a politician. Jesus wasn't doing miracles or preaching. And yet Simeon recognized that this baby was God's answer to many prayers.

How often do you recognize what God is doing in your life? It's hard to see things with God's eyes. Perhaps you've been sick. Or maybe a loved one has died. Is that God's plan?

During the hard times, it's difficult to have faith that God is still in control. Simeon stands out as a man of faith. Hebrews 11:1 says it this way,

day
eighteen

"Faith is being sure of what we hope for. It is being sure of what we do not see." The rest of Hebrews chapter 11 talks about people having faith in God during good times *and* hard times.

We need eyes to see what God has already done for us. And then we should join Simeon in praising God because "my eyes have seen your salvation" (Luke 2:30).

PRAYer:

Father, give me eyes to see how You move through my life.
I want to praise You for

_____.

(Fill in the blank with a specific thing He's done in your life!)

Creative Spark

Journal today about something God has done in your life. The fact that He cares about us is a thing of wonder!

·WONDER·

Create art that expresses
your wonder and joy.

WONDER & JOY

93

TALKING ABOUT JESUS

And [Anna] spoke about the child
to all who were looking forward to the time
when Jerusalem would be set free.
LUKE 2:38

YESTERDAY, we saw that Simeon waited for the Lord's Savior and then saw baby Jesus at the temple. Also in the temple was a prophetess named Anna. She was very old and never left the temple. She didn't have family to distract her. She'd been married, but her husband had died long before. She worshiped and prayed day and night.

When Mary and Joseph brought Jesus to the temple, Anna saw them. Like Simeon, she recognized that the baby was God's Savior to the world. Like Simeon, she gave thanks to God. But Luke says that she did one more thing. She started talking about the child. If anyone was interested in the Messiah, she told them about Jesus. She took the time to explain how this child was God's Messiah.

day 19

Remember, the shepherds had the same response! They told everyone they knew about what they had seen and heard.

Do you explain your faith to others? It's not complicated. You don't have to have all the answers. You don't need to be fancy about what you say. You just need to report what you saw and heard. The shepherds saw angels and a baby in a manger. Anna saw a baby in the temple. They all looked at the baby with wonder! They didn't have to explain Him. They just needed to tell others what they had seen with their own eyes.

PRAYer:

Today, Lord, help me explain
how Christmas is a thing of wonder
because Jesus is Your Son.
I want to talk about You!

Creative Spark

Journal some of the things you've learned about the baby Jesus. Telling others about Jesus doesn't mean you have to use big words or ideas. It can be as simple as saying, "Once, there was a special baby born. . ."

ONCE, THERE WAS A SPECIAL BABY BORN...

day 19

Create art that expresses what you want to share about Jesus with your friends and family. Is it His love, His comfort, His peace. . . ?

TALKING POINTS

The shepherds and Anna are examples of people who liked talking about Jesus. Take the time to list some "talking points." What are some things you could tell someone about Jesus?

Maybe it's a personal experience—something that really happened to you. It doesn't have to be a big event, just something God did in your life. Maybe you passed a test, or your dental appointment didn't hurt, or you got a hit in your baseball game. God cares about everything in your life. All you have to do is tell others about the small things God has done for you.

Create art that expresses a time when God showed up in your life. Think through how you might explain this to others.

HOW GOD SHOWED UP FOR ME...

the ROCKS, STONES AND STARS

We saw His star in the east.
We came to worship Him.
MATTHEW 2:2 ICB

ONE day, Jesus's disciples were praising God with loud voices and shouting that Jesus was the King of heaven. Some Pharisees didn't like that. They told Jesus to make His disciples stop.

Jesus had an interesting thing to say: "I tell you," He replied, "if they keep quiet, the stones will cry out" (Luke 19:40).

If the disciples stopped praising God, the stones—the earth itself—would have to shout about Jesus! We shouldn't be surprised by that. After all, God created and controls the universe, how the planets and stars move. Making stones cry out would be simple for God.

Likewise, it was simple for Him to move the stars around to show the wise men that our Savior was about to be born. The wise men from the east saw "His star." They came to Jerusalem to find the newborn king. "Where was He born?" they asked.

To answer the question, the chief priests and teachers of the law

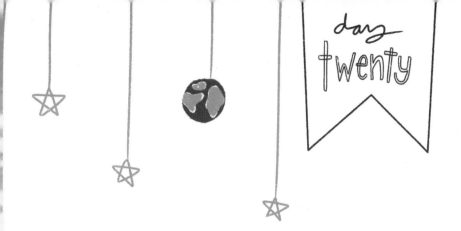

had to look at Old Testament prophecies. Finally, they figured out that the Christ, the Messiah, the Savior of their people, would be born in Bethlehem.

Amazingly, the wise men could have skipped Jerusalem and the teachers and priests, because the star "went ahead of them. It finally stopped over the place where the child was" (Matthew 2:9).

God chose to move the heavens to announce the birth of His Son!

PRAYer:

Father, I pray that the stones and rocks
never have to call out praise to You.
Instead, fill my heart and mouth with praise.

Creative Spark

Rocks, stones, and stars—they all praise God! As you journal today, let words of praise fill the lines below.

day
twenty

Draw, paint, and doodle everything you can think of that praises God. Rocks, stones, stars. . .

♥ THE WISE MEN'S GIFTS

When they saw the star,
they were filled with joy.
MATTHEW 2:10

YESTERDAY, we saw that Jesus's star brought the wise men to see Him. It's interesting to compare the reactions of the wise men and King Herod, the ruler of Judea.

The news about a newborn king disturbed King Herod and everyone in Jerusalem. King Herod called together all the religious leaders and asked where the newborn king was supposed to be born. In Bethlehem, they said.

King Herod probably saw this as a challenge to his throne. He told the wise men that he wanted to worship the newborn king too. He asked them to bring him information about the baby. He didn't plan to worship the new king, though. Instead, King Herod hoped to kill the baby so it would never grow up to be king.

The wise men, however, had a different response to Jesus. When they saw that the star had stopped, showing them where the baby lay, they "were filled with joy" (Matthew 2:10). They went into the

day 21

house and saw Mary with the baby Jesus. "They bowed down and worshiped Him. Then they opened their treasures. They gave Him gold, frankincense and myrrh" (Matthew 2:11).

King Herod feared the rise of another king. The wise men were full of joy, and they worshiped Jesus. They gave their best and most expensive gifts. Fear—or joy? What's your response to Jesus?

PRAYer:

Father, use me today
to bring people the good news
of Your gospel.

Creative Spark

God used a star to bring wise men to worship Jesus! What does God use in your community to bring people to Him? In the space below, write an outreach plan that will bring new people into your church. If there are Christmas parties or events scheduled, plan ways to help.

• OUTREACH •

day
☆ 21 ☆

Draw and write about the ways that people can find out about Jesus.

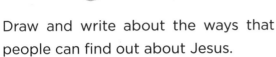

BE A giver

Then they opened their treasures.
They gave him gold, frankincense and myrrh.
MATTHEW 2:11

CHRISTMAS is all about getting and giving gifts, right?

The tradition of giving gifts can be traced back to the wise men, who brought gifts to the baby Jesus. They brought some of the most expensive gifts possible. But they also received a special gift: Jesus, who would save the world. Today, let's think about giving.

First, the wise men gave gold, a precious mineral that is expensive even today. Second, they gave frankincense. This was an incense or perfume that smelled good. Incense is often burned in religious ceremonies, so it points to Jesus's importance in religion. Often, the myrrh was an oil used to pour over or anoint someone. The anointing could mean that the person was dedicated to serving God or to confirm that they should be king.

These expensive treasures were meant for a king. They were a sign of respect, a sign that the wise men recognized the importance of this baby. Others who met baby Jesus, though, gave a different kind of gift. The shepherds took time away from their flocks and told everyone about the newborn King. Simeon and Anna had awaited the baby for years. When they finally saw Him, they gave Mary and Joseph the gift of words of encouragement.

Expensive or not, giving demands one thing: you, the giver, must think about who will receive the gift. For example, to find the right gift for your grandmother, you must think about her and what she likes. Giving means giving of your time, energy, or creativity. That's the way to find the perfect gift.

PRAYer:

Father, thank You for the gift
of my Savior, Jesus.
No other gift can compare.
Teach me to be a giver of special gifts.

Creative Spark

Christmas is in just a couple of days. You've probably already done your gift shopping. Today's challenge, though, is to be creative in thinking about extra-special gifts for those you love. Here are some gift ideas for you to journal about and plan: Healing words. Apologies. Prayers that act as a gift. A long visit with time to really talk. The gift of doing chores for someone. The gift of listening. The gift of babysitting. The gift of cooking together. These are just some ways you could give. Write your list below.

day 22

Create a scene of how you're going to give someone a creative, special gift this season.

PLANNING GIFTS

Giving of your time is one of the best gifts. Plan to spend an hour with someone. What "gift" can you give them in an hour's time? Examples are the gift of listening, a gift of cooking together, or a gift of babysitting so someone has an hour to do something they love.

BONUS

Journal and create art about giving and gifts.

ESCAPE

Joseph got up. During the night,
he left for Egypt with the Child
and His mother Mary.
MATTHEW 2:14

WHEN the wise men came to Judea in search of the newborn King of the Jews, they stopped first in Jerusalem. There, they talked with King Herod, the ruler of Judea. He said, "Go and search carefully for the child. As soon as you find Him, report it to me. Then I can go and worship Him too" (Matthew 2:8).

Of course, King Herod didn't want to worship baby Jesus! Instead, he wanted to kill Him to prevent Him from growing up to be a king. It was a dangerous time for Joseph, Mary, and Jesus. Fortunately, God had plans.

God's plan started with a message to the wise men: "But God warned them in a dream not to go back to Herod. So they returned to their country on a different road" (Matthew 2:12). God made sure that King Herod didn't get any information about Jesus.

Still, Herod knew that there was a baby boy somewhere in

the area. God sent an angel to Joseph in a dream. "'Get up!' the angel said. 'Take the child and His mother and escape to Egypt. Stay there until I tell you to come back. Herod is going to search for the child. He wants to kill Him.'" (Matthew 2:13).

Joseph obeyed! He took Mary and Jesus to Egypt and stayed there until King Herod died. It was hard to go to Egypt because it was a different country with a different language and a different culture. Joseph had to find work in this strange country. Living away from family would have been hard too. Remember, Mary had already given birth away from her family. Grandparents and other family still wouldn't be nearby to babysit or help raise the child.

Obeying God in this situation meant escaping bad times. Jesus was safe from King Herod. But obedience isn't always easy. It meant a couple of hard years for Mary and Joseph.

PRAYer:

Lord, thank You that You have a plan for me to avoid trouble and evil. Give me faith to obey when You ask me to do something hard.

Journal about following God even when it's hard. Think about the difference between these two things: Easy but Wrong; Hard but Right.

Create art that expresses a scene from your life. When have you been obedient even though it would have been easier to take a different path?

CONTENTMENT

*"I serve the Lord," Mary answered.
"May it happen to me just as you said it would."*
LUKE 1:38

CONTENTMENT is being happy exactly where God put you. An angel visited Mary with startling news: even though you're not married, you'll have a baby. Mary argued about it, but the angel said, "The Word of God will never fail" (Luke 1:37 NLT).

Mary only had two choices: be angry or be happy.

Mary could've been angry about many things. She was engaged to Joseph and probably looking forward to a big wedding. Babies were a lot of work. Her hopes and dreams had to change.

Her response is startling. "I serve the Lord," Mary answered.

She put God's will for her life above everything else. She changed her expectations to meet God's plans for her life. Her attitude was "Bring it on."

She started the adventure of faith—being the mother of our Savior—with an attitude of contentment.

Her attitude is one that we need when we open our Christmas

gifts. There's a real danger as we are swept up in the fun of the gifts. What if you don't get the gifts you anticipated? What if you get something less, something smaller, something cheaper?

You have only two choices: be angry or be happy.

Fill your heart with Mary's joy and contentment. Choose happiness. Choose to be thankful for anything and everything God brings your way. You've already received the best gift the universe can give: a Savior, who is Christ the Lord.

PRAYER:

Father, thank You for putting me
in the perfect place at the perfect time.
Teach me to be content right where You put me.

CREATIVE SPARK

Journal about contentment. Think about your situation—whatever it is—and thank God for His plan for your life.

Create art that shows ways to express your gratefulness this season. Maybe a thank-you note or a hug, or you could even volunteer to help clean up.

WONDER

We love because He loved us first.
I JOHN 4:19

THE birth of Jesus was foretold way back in Genesis. When Adam and Eve sinned by eating the forbidden fruit, they were separated from God. As a holy God, He couldn't have anything to do with sin. Otherwise, He wouldn't be holy any longer. There was nothing Adam and Eve could do to have a relationship with God again.

But God could do something. He promised that a Savior would come. To the serpent who tricked Adam and Eve, God said, "I will make you and the woman hate each other. Your children and her children will be enemies. Her son will crush your head" (Genesis 3:15).

The rest of the Old Testament is about waiting for Jesus. God chooses the Israelite people, and they disobey over and over. Still, God loves His people. He wants a relationship with them. God put on an incredible show: angel messengers, a miracle birth, obedient stars, evil kings, wise men with gold, a host of heavenly angels, and a rescue. Wow! It's a wondrous story.

And it's the fulfillment, the completion, of the entire Old Testament. Everything was leading up to this one child. At the perfect time, God sent His Son as a Savior. When Jesus died on the cross, He took the punishment for the sins of everyone. The sin was covered up as if it never happened. That means the holy God could again have a relationship with His people.

The wonder of Christmas is partly the amazing things that happened leading up to Jesus's birth. We are awed by the angels and the miracles. But the real wonder is that God reached down to us in love.

PRAYER:

O Lord, Creator of the heavens and the earth,
who am I that You should take notice of me?
And yet, Lord, You sent Your Son—Your only Son—
to save me from my sin. Thank You.

Creative Spark

Ponder God's love and the wonder of
Christmas. Write about it.

Create a Christmas scene.

WHAT CHRISTMAS MEANS TO ME

It's been an exciting and fun month studying and journaling about the Christmas story. Review your journaling. Think about what you've learned and what you've been able to express through your art. Merry Christmas!

BONUS

This is your space to express your wonder and awe at the birth of our Savior.

Dear Friend,

This book was prayerfully crafted with you, the reader, in mind—every word, every sentence, every page—was thoughtfully written, designed, and packaged to encourage you...right where you are this very moment. At DaySpring, our vision is to see every person experience the life-changing message of God's love. So, as we worked through rough drafts, design changes, edits and details, we prayed for you to deeply experience His unfailing love, indescribable peace, and pure joy. It is our sincere hope that through these Truth-filled pages your heart will be blessed, knowing that God cares about you—your desires and disappointments, your challenges and dreams.

He knows. He cares. He loves you unconditionally.

BLESSINGS!
THE DAYSPRING BOOK TEAM

———————————

Additional copies of this book and
other DaySpring titles can be purchased
at fine bookstores everywhere.
Order online at dayspring.com
or
by phone at 1-877-751-4347